Science
Time

By Jean Warren
Illustrated by Susan True

Publisher: Roberta Suid
Editor: Bonnie Bernstein
Design: David Hale
Cover art: Corbin Hillam

ISBN 0-912107-18-9

Printed in the United States of America

9 8 7 6 5 4 3 2 1

PREFACE

Childhood is a time for exploring. Parents and teachers can support their young children's explorations and help them learn about their physical environment in many simple ways; for example, by calling attention to everyday learning situations (a bee on a flower, a rainfall, a stone sinking in a pond), by providing materials or together building devices that can extend a learning situation, and by encouraging children to find out "why" about all that they observe.

Science Time is a collection of activities for helping adults help children learn about their world. Like any science text, this book provides the simple facts and explanations children will need to understand the basics of their scientific inquiry. But the activities are designed more to emphasize the **process** involved in making scientific discoveries, rather than the discoveries themselves. Various activities will teach the children how to measure, compare, sort, predict, anticipate, estimate, and classify — skills that are as important to learn as new facts. The materials required are inexpensive and readily available in the home or classroom.

The activities in this book were compiled from ideas featured in the Totline, a 24-page bi-monthly newsletter. The Totline regularly features preschool activities in the following areas: art, creative movement, coordination, language development, learning games, science, and self-awareness. Each issue also includes holiday party ideas, sugarless snack recipes, and a special infant-toddler ideas section. For more information, write: Warren Publishing House, P.O. Box 2255, Everett, WA 98203.

CONTENTS

FALL & WINTER

Signs of Fall

Help your children notice signs of fall—what you observe will depend on where you live. Some general signs are:

- People buy or make warmer clothes, pile wood, and rake leaves.
- Some animals store food, grow thicker fur, and hibernate or fly south.
- Many plant leaves change their color and fall to the ground; foods ripen and are harvested.
- The soil gets harder, daylight is shorter, and the air temperature gets cooler.

All About Trees

Help your children become more aware of the trees in their environment. Let them observe different kinds of trees, comparing their general shapes and the shapes of their leaves. Do they have leaves or needles, fruit or nuts? Is the bark rough or smooth, peeling, thin or thick?

Ask the children to think of reasons why animals like trees. Here are a few possible answers: The leaves are food for insects; branches serve as anchors on which spiders can attach their webs; hollow trunks shelter small animals; fruits or nuts are good food for many animals; birds use trees to build their nests.

Talk about the ways that trees help people. For example, trees cool you on a hot day and protect you on a windy day. The roots keep the soil from washing away. Fruits and nuts that grow on trees are good food. Trees provide wood to build our houses and burn in our fireplaces.

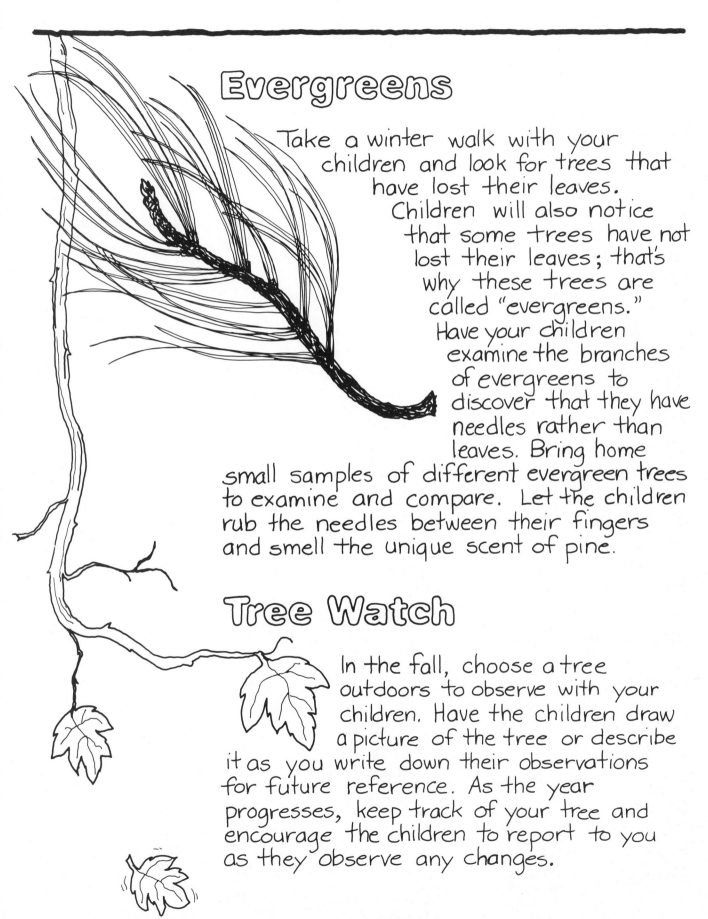

Evergreens

Take a winter walk with your children and look for trees that have lost their leaves. Children will also notice that some trees have not lost their leaves; that's why these trees are called "evergreens." Have your children examine the branches of evergreens to discover that they have needles rather than leaves. Bring home small samples of different evergreen trees to examine and compare. Let the children rub the needles between their fingers and smell the unique scent of pine.

Tree Watch

In the fall, choose a tree outdoors to observe with your children. Have the children draw a picture of the tree or describe it as you write down their observations for future reference. As the year progresses, keep track of your tree and encourage the children to report to you as they observe any changes.

Zoo Outing

As the days get cooler, bundle up your children and take a trip to the zoo. Most of us tend to go during the warmer months and miss some of the more fascinating animals who stay inside their caves and shelters where it is cooler.

The zoo is also a great place for observing signs of fall — seasonal vegetation, leaves changing colors, squirrels gathering nuts, animals' fur growing thicker and sometimes changing colors.

Seed Collection

Fall is a good time to begin a seed collection. Help your children discover seeds inside fruits and vegetables. Encourage them to start their own seed collection. Seeds should be washed, dried, and placed inside small plastic sandwich bags. Staple to the top of each bag a picture of what the seed is from (or could become).

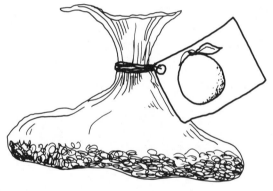

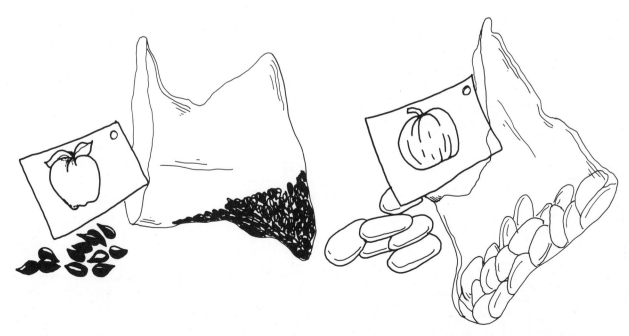

Harvest Poster

Materials: a large piece of paper, some old magazines, paste.

1. Help your children cut or tear out pictures of unprepared foods (fruits and vegetables).
2. Discuss the difference between prepared foods and food as it appears when it is first harvested.
3. Have your children paste the pictures on the large sheet of paper.
4. Hang the harvest poster in a convenient place and spend a few minutes each day with your child naming the different kinds of fruits and vegetables.

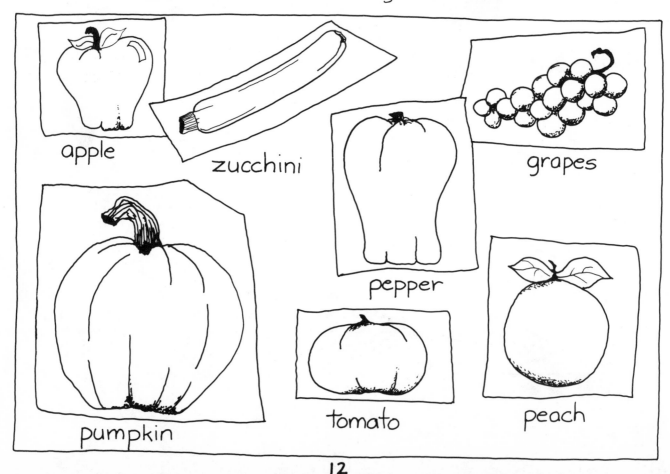

apple

zucchini

grapes

pepper

pumpkin

tomato

peach

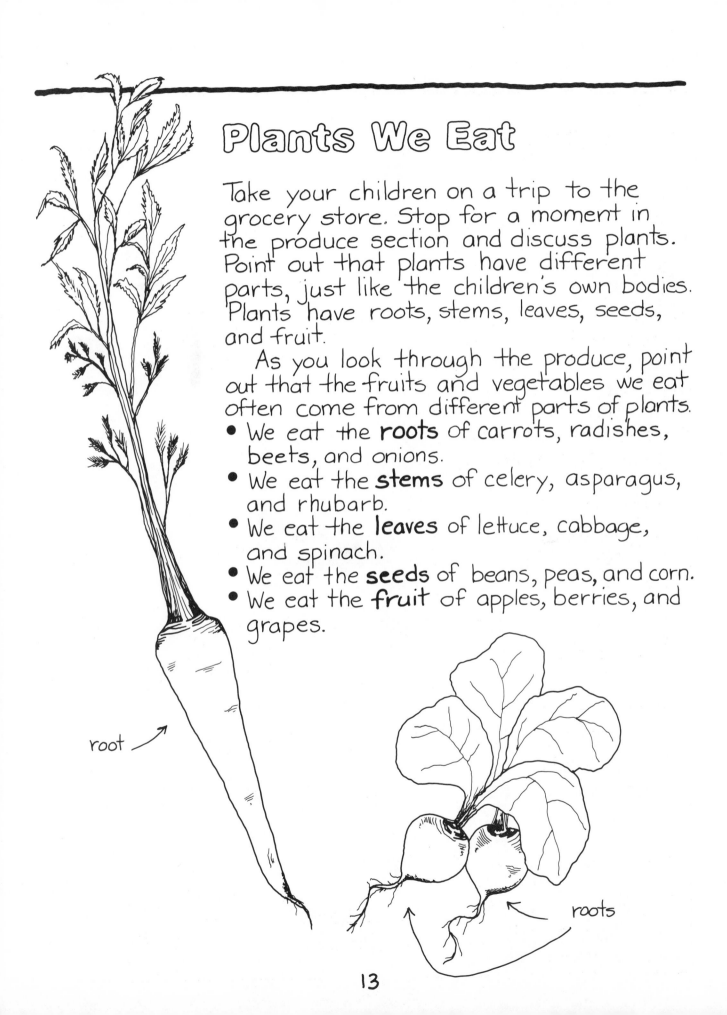

Plants We Eat

Take your children on a trip to the grocery store. Stop for a moment in the produce section and discuss plants. Point out that plants have different parts, just like the children's own bodies. Plants have roots, stems, leaves, seeds, and fruit.

As you look through the produce, point out that the fruits and vegetables we eat often come from different parts of plants.

- We eat the **roots** of carrots, radishes, beets, and onions.
- We eat the **stems** of celery, asparagus, and rhubarb.
- We eat the **leaves** of lettuce, cabbage, and spinach.
- We eat the **seeds** of beans, peas, and corn.
- We eat the **fruit** of apples, berries, and grapes.

root

roots

13

Dissecting Apples

Show your children three apples—one red, one green, and one yellow. Ask them to name the colors. Then discuss how they are all apples despite their different colors.

Take a knife and cut each one open side-ways. Point out how the seeds inside form a star. Discuss how the apples are all different on the outside, yet the same on the inside.

Turn your discussion to people. Talk about how people, like apples, are all different on the outside, yet the same on the inside.

Learning With Apples

Counting: Divide apples in halves or fourths. Let your children decide how many apples will be needed for everyone to receive a piece.

Counting: When you cut open an apple, let your children count the number of seeds inside.

Feeling: Place three different fruits—such as an orange, a banana, and an apple— in a bag. Let your children touch each fruit without looking in the bag. Can they identify the apple by its characteristics?

Smelling: Cut open three different fruits. Have your children close their eyes and try to identify each by its smell.

Personalized Pumpkins

If you are lucky enough to live where you can grow pumpkins, your children can grow pumpkins with their names on them. When the pumpkins are small and green, about the size of a grapefruit, help the children scratch their names into the rind of the pumpkin with a nail or small knife. As the pumpkin grows, the scratch will leave a scar that stands out.

Signs of Winter

Have your children help you look for signs of winter where you live. Examples:

Weather: Cold weather brings ice and snow. Daylight is short. Sometimes it is still dark when we get up in the morning.

Plants and Animals: All but the evergreen trees are bare. Many animals are gone, some flying south and some hibernating. The fur of some animals changes color to camouflage them in the snow.

People: We wear heavier clothing. We take out our gloves, boots, and hats. We play inside more. Many people have fires in their fireplaces. We play in the snow and must shovel our walkways.

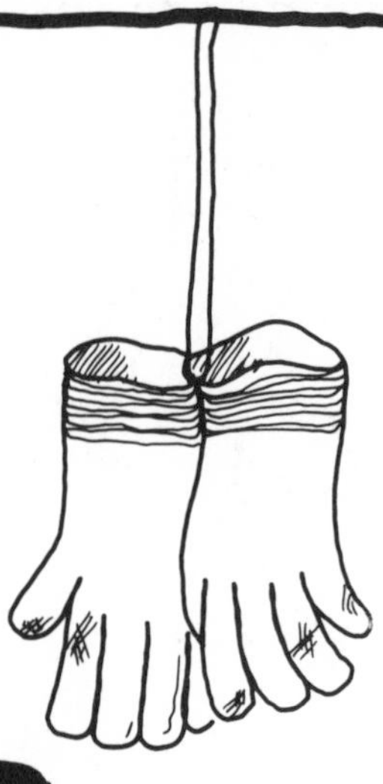

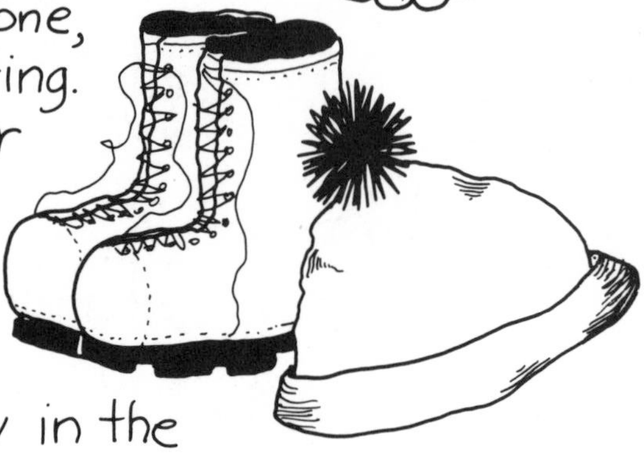

Sounds of Winter

Go on a winter walk. Listen for sounds of winter. Examples:

> boots crunching in snow
> rain splashing
> wind whistling

An interesting aspect of winter sounds is the relative **lack** of sounds. Many birds are gone and snow makes the world seem more quiet.

Bird Watching

Winter time can be a fun time to watch birds. Help your children make a bird feeder by cutting a large window in a plastic bottle or milk carton. Fill it with bread crumbs or birdseed and set it out where your children can observe it from indoors.

Birds also enjoy pine cones or toilet paper rolls that have been spread with peanut butter and rolled in birdseeds and hung out for them. Have your children hang them on trees so the birds can eat while resting on a branch.

use large plastic bottles

cut a large window

fill with bread crumbs or bird seed

Water Cycle Experiment

To help children understand the principles of evaporation, fill a large jar with ice cubes and put a lid on it. Soon little drops of water will appear on the outside of the jar. Where did the water drops come from? Offer this explanation: When water is **heated** it changes from a **liquid** to a **vapor** and rises into the air. When water vapor in the air is **cooled** it changes back to a **liquid**.

Examples of evaporation: tea pot steaming, clothes drying.

Examples of condensation: water on windows and mirrors, rain.

Insulation Experiment

Children can study the basics of insulation by wrapping ice cubes in different materials and seeing which ones melt first. Different wrapping materials include: tissue paper, aluminum foil, styrofoam packing material, plastic wrap, a wool scarf, or a wash rag. This project should raise many questions and observations which you will want to explore with your children:

ice cube wrapped in tissue

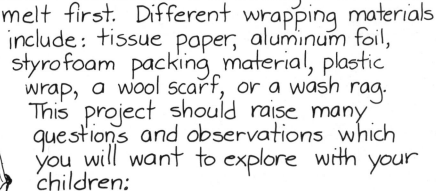

- What kinds of things are insulated in their homes?
  - Why are some materials better insulators than others?
  - What are some natural insulators?
  - Why do we want to keep some things cold and some things hot?

You and the children could look for pictures of things that are insulated in magazines and put them together in book form.

foil

Christmas Scene Shapes

Create a shape scene on a felt board, chalkboard, or large piece of paper. Make the objects in the scene definite shapes. Here are some examples for a Christmas scene:

> triangle tree
> circle tree ornaments
> circle clock on wall
> square and rectangle presents
> square or rectangle window

Play a game with your children by calling out the name of a shape and having them point to an object in the scene that has that shape. As an extension, discuss shapes with your children and have them look around your room and find shapes.

Star of David

While discussing shapes with young children, show them how they can make a Star of David by placing an inverted triangle on top of an upright triangle. Then try this project.

Materials: 6 popsicle sticks, glue, glitter.

1. Glue together two triangles made up of three popsicle sticks each.
2. Turn one triangle upside down and glue it on top of the other to make a Star of David.
3. Have your children spread glue on the sticks and then sprinkle them with glitter. If you put glitter on both sides, you can hang three or four triangles together for a spectacular mobile.

glue

All About Lights

The holidays are a good time to discuss different kinds of lights with young children—how we can enjoy them but also how we must be very careful around them.

Sources of light: sun, electric bulbs, fire.

Good things about lights: Lights provide heat and allow us to see things in the dark. We can cook things with fire. Candles and colored lights are pretty.

Dangers about lights: Too much sun can burn us. Light bulbs can become too hot to touch. Playing with electrical cords or sockets can result in getting an electrical shock. We should not get too close to fire, including candles, because it could ignite our clothes.

Candle Holders

You and your children can make a pretty holiday candle holder.

Materials: small empty can (soup size is fine), hammer, nail, candle.

1. Clean out a small tin can and fill it with water.

2. Freeze the water, then let the children help you hammer nail holes around the outside of the can. (The ice holds the sides of the can firm.)

3. Let the ice melt and pour out the water. Place a candle in the bottom of the can and light it. Holders look great in a dark room.

Name That Bell

Beg or borrow three or four different types of bells, for example, a sleigh bell, dinner bell, cow bell, and a bird cage bell. Let your children play with the bells.

Encourage them to listen to the unique sound each bell makes. Help them come up with a name to distinguish each bell.

Play a game with your children. Have them turn around or hide their eyes. Ring one of the bells and see if they can tell you which bell was rung.

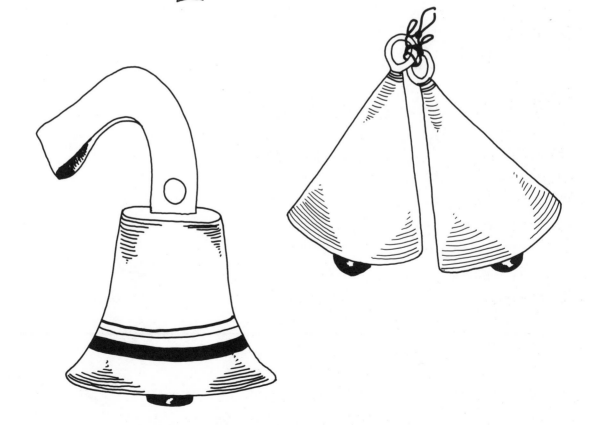

Snow Gauge

Help your children make a snow gauge.
Materials: a large empty coffee can, ruler, marking pen (permanent ink).
1. Place the ruler inside the can. Mark and number inches onto the inside of the can.
2. When it snows, place the can outside in a clear place.
3. When it stops snowing, you and your children can tell how deep the snow is by noting which inch mark it has reached.

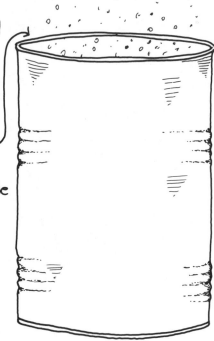

mark inches on inside of can

Snow Tracks

Encourage your children to be snow detectives by looking for tracks in the snow and trying to identify who made the tracks. Examples:

dog tracks
cat tracks
people tracks
bird tracks
other animal tracks

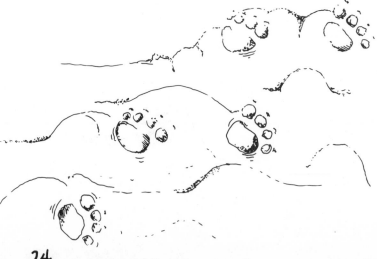

Snowflakes

If it snows where you live, let your children examine snowflakes with a magnifying glass. They should note that snowflakes are frozen water crystals and each flake is unique with its own design.

A good way to catch snowflakes for examination is to set out a piece of cardboard covered with dark felt. Place your felt board in the freezer before setting it out to catch snowflakes. Snowflakes will last longer before melting on the cold board.

Shadow Record

1:00

February 2nd is Ground Hog Day. According to legend, on this day a ground hog awakens from his winter nap and looks outside his hole. If the sun is shining and he sees his shadow, he is frightened and he returns to his home in the ground, indicating there will be six more weeks of winter. If the day is cloudy and the groundhog does not see his shadow, he stays out and plays, indicating the arrival of spring.

2:00

Take advantage of the day and talk about shadows. When you stand in front of the sun, your body blocks the light and creates a shadow. The position of the sun in the sky affects the length of your shadow.

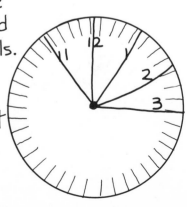

3:00

Find a short tree or object outside to observe on a sunny day. Each hour help your children measure the length of the object's shadow and make a picture record.

Shadow Clock

On a sunny day, take a paper plate outside and punch a pencil down through the center, into the ground. Have the children watch a regular clock and every hour mark the plate where the shadow falls. If it is one o'clock, mark the shadow line with **1** and so on each hour.

Leave the plate in the same spot and the next day the children won't need a regular clock to tell the time. They can tell the time by the pencil's shadow.

SPRING & SUMMER

Signs of Spring

Take your children on a walk in early spring. Have them observe signs of spring along the way. For example, buds are beginning to bloom—in fact, there already may be flowers. Birds are returning and building nests. The trees have new branches and new leaves.

Smells and Sounds of Spring

While you and your children are playing outside, discover the sounds and smells of spring. For example, **smell** the fresh air, mown grass, flowers, and moist soil. Hear the sounds of birds, people working outside, lawnmowers, and children at play.

Blooming Buds

Go for a nature walk and look for new bud growth. If it's feasible, bring back a couple of branches. Place them in water in a warm place. Let your children observe the buds opening.

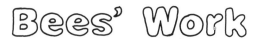

Bees' Work

Flowers are always happy to have their friends the bees visit because they always bring a gift of pollen. Flowers need the pollen to help form new flower seeds.

Late spring and early summer are good times to examine flowers. Show your children the powdery pollen on the tips of the stamens. Explain how as the bee flies from one flower to another, he gets pollen from one flower on his feet which rubs off onto the next flower he visits. Sometimes the wind blows pollen from flower to flower, but the bees do a better job.

The bee, of course, enjoys visiting the flowers because the flowers produce a sweet nectar which the bees love to drink. The bee flies deep into the flower to get the nectar. The bee later uses the nectar to make honey. Bees make honey during the summer to eat during the winter. After your walk, give the children a snack of honey and apples.

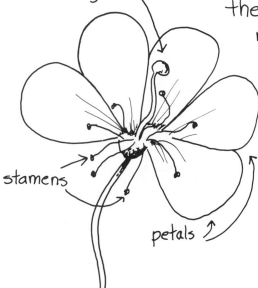

stigma

stamens

petals

Belly and Back Exploring

When you are outside with your children, have them lay on their stomachs and explore what they can see from that perspective, then have them turn over on their backs and explore what they see up above.

Scientific questions may arise that children can investigate. This activity can also lead to imaginative play. For example, the children can develop stories about tiny animals that live in the grass or under the dirt, or name objects they see in cloud formations.

Nature Collections

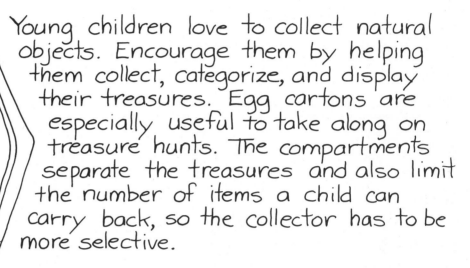

Young children love to collect natural objects. Encourage them by helping them collect, categorize, and display their treasures. Egg cartons are especially useful to take along on treasure hunts. The compartments separate the treasures and also limit the number of items a child can carry back, so the collector has to be more selective.

Thermometer Reading

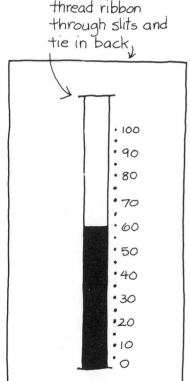

thread ribbon through slits and tie in back

Spring is a good time to help children learn how to read a thermometer. Obtain a large outdoor thermometer and place it on a level where young children can read it easily. Then make a play thermometer that they can manipulate themselves.

Materials: Piece of cardboard, red crayon or marker, white ribbon twice as long as the cardboard.

1. Cut a small slit at the top and bottom of the piece of cardboard.
2. Color half the ribbon red.
3. Thread the ribbon through the slits and tie the ends together in the back.
4. Mark the front of the cardboard with the degree calibrations found on a real thermometer.
5. As the children observe the temperature changes during the day on the real thermometer, have them adjust their make-believe thermometer by moving the red ribbon up or down.

Observing Birds

Encourage your children to observe the birds in your area. Talk about the many different kinds of birds there are, and ask the children to look for birds of different sizes and colors. If you're lucky, you and your children may be able to watch different birds eat different kinds of food and build different kinds of nests.

What do birds eat? Some eat insects, seeds, ripe fruits and vegetables, flower nectar, tree sap, worms, and small animals.

Bird Nest Garden

What do birds use to build their nests? Grass, weeds, moss, mud, twigs, flower petals, hair, feathers, and human litter they find scattered about—cotton, string, paper, rags, wood shavings, foil, yarn.

If you ever happen to find a vacant bird's nest, let your children take turns watering it each day. It won't be long before grass and flowers sprout.

Bird Nest Bag

Help your children collect bright-colored items that birds can use to build their nests. Examples include yarn, thread, ribbons, strips of plastic or fabrics, hair, feathers.

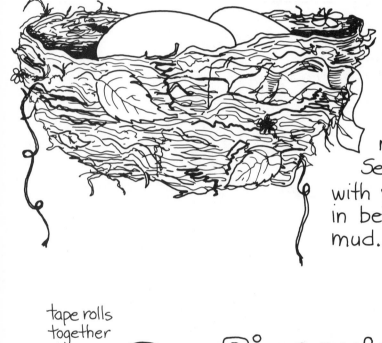

Place all items in a mesh onion bag and tie it at the top. Hang the bag in a nearby tree and watch the contents slowly disappear.

In a few weeks, go on a nature walk with your children. See if you can spot any bird nests with your colorful items tucked in between the grass, twigs, and mud.

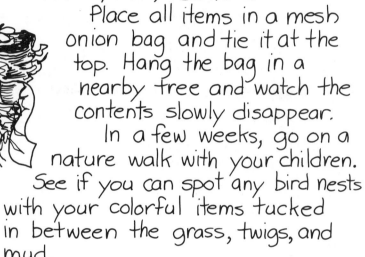

tape rolls together

Binoculars

You can make your children a pair of make-believe binoculars by taping together two toilet paper rolls. A piece of yarn or string can be used to make a neck strap. This simple toy is great for investigating the birds that live in your area.

attach yarn or string for neck strap

Insect Investigation

Children seem to love to gather, examine, and usually bring indoors a variety of insects. Take advantage of their natural curiosity and help them collect four or five different insects for observation.

Help them observe these differences: Some are big; some are small. Some have wings; some do not.

Help them observe these similarities: All have six legs, three body parts, and two antennae.

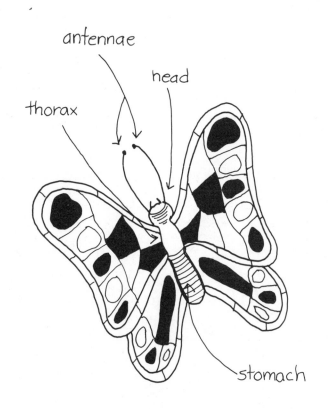

antennae

head

thorax

stomach

Bug Keeper

Materials: 2 plastic spray can lids, soft wire screening approximately 7"x9".

1. Roll the screening into a cylinder that fits snugly into one of the lids.
2. Sew or wire the screening together. Any remaining sharp edges should be covered with masking tape.
3. Put a lid on one end. Then, after you've caught a bug, put the second lid on the other end.

When keeping insects, remember that they are fun to watch for a couple of days but then they should be let go.

Caterpillar Life Cycle

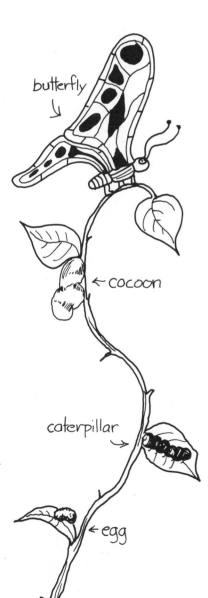

butterfly

← cocoon

caterpillar

← egg

Observing the life cycle of a caterpillar is a good way to learn about the life of an insect. Like all insects, caterpillars go through four distinct life stages:

1. the egg
2. the larva (as a caterpillar, the insect eats and eats)
3. the pupa (in a cocoon the caterpillar sleeps and slowly changes)
4. the adult (a butterfly or moth emerges from the cocoon)

If your children happen to find a caterpillar in the yard, have them place it in a jar or bug keeper. Suggest that they put in some leaves, like those they saw it feeding upon. With luck, the children will be able to observe the caterpillar spinning a cocoon and later emerging from it.

Bubble Solutions

Children love making bubbles. A good solution for making large bubbles is to mix 3/4 cup of liquid soap with 1/4 cup of glycerine and 2 quarts of water. Glycerine can be obtained at the drug store. Place the solution in a large shallow pan.

Children dip a bubble maker into the bubble solution and then wave the bubble maker through the air, creating giant bubbles.

Bubble Blowers

Dip larger end into solution, blow through hole.

Poke a hole in the bottom of a paper cup.

Cut a straw about an inch at one end. Bend strips back, dip in solution, and blow through other end.

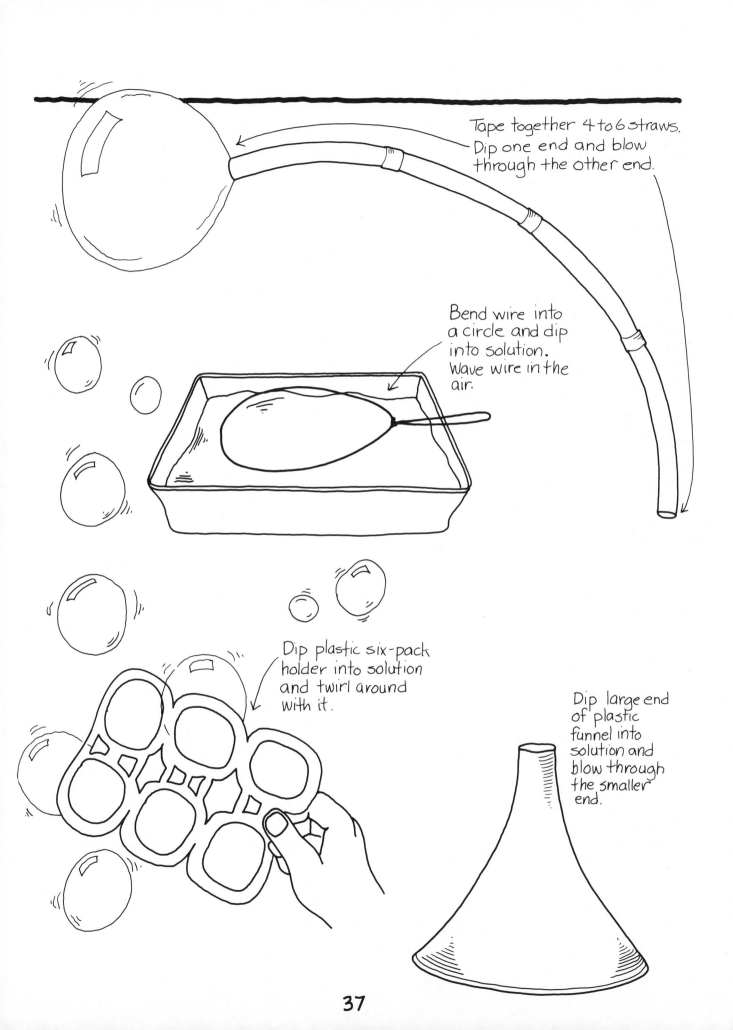

Tape together 4 to 6 straws. Dip one end and blow through the other end.

Bend wire into a circle and dip into solution. Wave wire in the air.

Dip plastic six-pack holder into solution and twirl around with it.

Dip large end of plastic funnel into solution and blow through the smaller end.

Easter Feelies

Children can celebrate Easter by enjoying how objects associated with the holiday **feel**. Set out some Easter objects and encourage the children to feel them and describe the sensations. Here are examples:

bunnies — **soft**
cooked eggs — **hard**
baskets — **scratchy**
plastic eggs — **smooth**

Dyeing Eggs

Give young children food coloring rather than colored tablets that come in dyeing kits to dye their Easter eggs. This will give them an opportunity to experiment with mixing colors and to discover how secondary colors are made. Have them mix yellow and blue to make green; red and blue to make purple; and yellow and red to make orange.

experiment by mixing colors

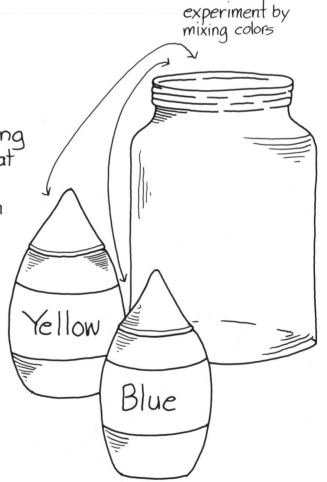

Plant Health

Have your children put some dirt in a plastic cup. Give them some seeds to plant and discuss why it is important to water plants and set them in the sun.

As an experiment, have the children plant seeds in two cups. Then have them set the cups in the sun, but only water one of the plants. Ask the children to observe what happens. As a second part of the experiment, have the children plant seeds in another two cups, water both cups, but then place one cup in the sun and the other one in a dark place. Discuss what they observe happens.

A discussion of healthy plants could easily lead into a discussion of healthy people. Like plants, people need certain things to grow healthy and strong. See if your children can help you think of what they might be: food, water, shelter, sunshine, exercise and love.

Thirsty Plants

Have your children mix some food coloring in a glass of water. Place a celery stalk in the water. Watch what happens in a few days.

Watering Plants

If you have plants around the room or house, let your children help you with the watering by giving them a clean spray bottle filled with water. Children love spraying.

Sprout Garden Bags

Children can grow sprouts in sandwich-size zip-lock plastic bags.

Materials: A zip-lock bag for each child, large needle, seeds (alfalfa or mung beans), bowl of warm water.

1. Punch about 10 holes in the bottom of the bag with a large needle. Be sure that some holes are on the bottom seam so that water will drain well from the bag.
2. Have your children fill their bags 1/8 to 1/4 full with seeds.
3. Next, zip up the bag and place it in a bowl of warm water. Soak the seeds like this overnight.
4. The next day, drain the seeds well and place them in a light place, but not in direct sunlight. For the next 3 or 4 days have your children rinse and drain their seeds daily.
5. Place the sprouted seeds in direct sunlight on the last day and they will green up more. Store sprouts in the same bag in the refrigerator. They should stay fresh for a week or two.

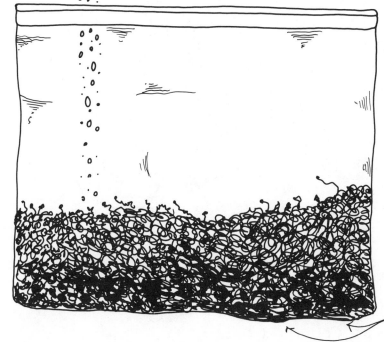

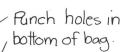

Punch holes in bottom of bag.

Carrot Top Garden

Cut the tops off of three or four carrots. Have your children place them in a shallow dish and water them daily. The carrot tops should be sitting in 1/4-inch water at all times.

Sit back and watch your carrot tops sprout new beautiful green foliage. Children especially love "planting" carrot tops because the greens sprout quickly and they are quite attractive.

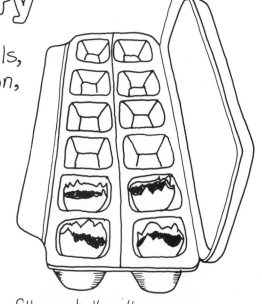

Egg Carton Nursery

Materials: Egg carton, 12 half eggshells, potting soil, marigold seeds, teaspoon, water.

1. Let your children fill an egg carton with empty halves of egg shells.
2. Have them fill each shell with potting soil and carefully plant one or two marigold seeds in each shell.
3. Water each shell with a teaspoon of water. Seeds will sprout more quickly if the lid of the egg carton is kept closed so that the seeds will stay warm.
4. When the seeds sprout, have the children replant the seedlings outside, crushing each shell as they place it into the ground.

fill egg shells with potting soil

Personal Terrarium

Materials: 2 clear plastic cups per child (sundae containers from McDonald's work great), clear cellophane tape or glue, dirt, rocks, wood chips, small plants or weeds.

1. Have the children each fill one plastic cup up half way.
2. Let them plant some small plants or weeds and stick in a rock or wood chip as landscape.
3. Place another cup on top and tape or glue the two cups together.

Terrariums are self-watering and are fascinating to watch as the water evaporates, then condenses, and finally rains down on the plants.

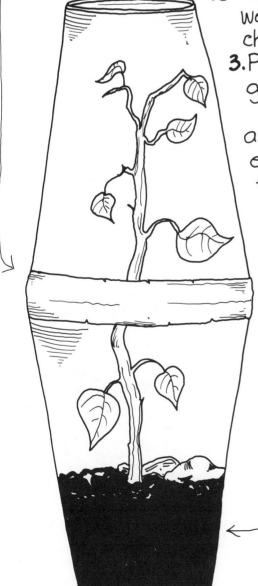

tape or glue cups together

fill cup with dirt and add rocks or wood chips

Grass Seed Starters

The quickest and easiest seeds to grow are grass or alfalfa. They tend to grow almost anywhere as long as they are watered regularly and have sunlight. Below are some unusual planters.

Cut sponge, sprinkle on seeds and water.

carve face ↘

Slice off top, scoop out potato, add cotton, water, and sprinkle with seeds.

Slice off bottom of potato.

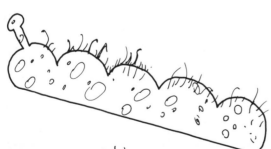

Cut sponge, sprinkle on seeds and water.

Fill cup with dirt, decorate to resemble a face, sprinkle seeds and water. Watch person's hair grow.

Grass Expedition

Take your children on a science expedition in the yard. Let them explore the grass and see what different kinds of plants and animals they can find.

Have the children collect samples of as many different kinds of plants as they can find. This will usually include such things as moss, clover, dandelions, crab grass, and tall wheat-type grasses. Check out some science books at your local library and help your children identify the plants, weeds, and grasses in your yard.

Have your children examine dandelion leaves and see if they can tell how the plant got its name, which in French means "teeth of the lion."

Soil Investigation

Examine dirt found in your yard with your children. Use your eyes, fingers, noses, and a good magnifying glass. You should discover that dirt is made out of small pieces of rock (sand) and decaying matter from plants and animals.

　　See if you can find two different kinds of dirt in your yard or elsewhere. Have your children compare the dirts looking for differences. Which dirt would be best for growing plants? (Plants will grow in sand, but they will grow bigger and stronger in dirt that has nutrients from decaying plant and animal life. They have trouble growing in clay soils because there is poor drainage.)

Dirt Safari

Dig up a couple of cupfuls of dirt. Dump them onto a newspaper that has been spread out on the floor and let your children examine the dirt to see what animals, plants, or rocks they can find. Small sifters or magnifying glasses are useful tools to help search through a pile of dirt.

Sand Study

What is sand? Show your children some rocks or shells and some sand. See if they can tell you where sand comes from. Why do you find sand at the beach? Explain that powerful waves smash rocks and shells into tiny pieces. The water keeps the pieces clean. We call the pieces sand. When rocks break down into tiny pieces and mix with decayed plants, we call it dirt.

Sand is fun to play with. See if your children can help you think of things that you can do with dry sand and wet sand. Explore the effect of water upon the characteristics of the sand.

Sand Combs

Cut out large cardboard combs for your children to play with in the sand.

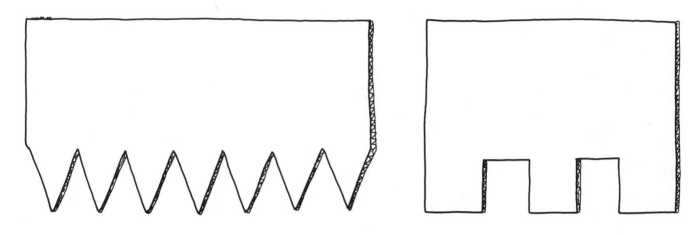

Sand Scoops

Make a scoop for your child to play with at the beach or in the sand box. Cut away the bottom from a bleach bottle or other round plastic bottle.

cut bottle

Sand Dolls

Sand dolls are fun to fill and play with on the beach or in the sandbox. Make a regular drawstring tote bag, then sew up the middle of the inside of the bottom of the bag to give the appearance of two fat legs. Turn the bag right side out again and draw a face on the top half of the bag with permanent marking pens. The child takes the doll to the beach or sandbox and fills it with sand, plays with the doll, and then simply dumps out the sand when it is time to go home.

draw a face

sew up middle of bag

Footprints in the Sand

Provide your children with a fun sand experience. Take them to a sandy beach or a park with a sandbox. Have them make footprints in damp sand. Pour plaster of Paris into the foot impressions and make a cast of everyone's foot.

If you end up with a number of different-sized footprints or handprints, use them to demonstrate to children that they are growing at different rates and that the size of their hands and feet will continue to grow as they get older.

All About Wind

What is wind? Moving air.

How do we know when it is windy? We can see wind move things; we can feel it on our faces.

What are some things we can see the wind move? Sailboats, kites, smoke, leaves, clouds, clothes, flags.

How can the wind help us? The wind moves boats, turns windmills, and dries clothes.

How can the wind hurt us? Wind can blow down trees and power lines.

How do we protect ourselves from the wind? We wear clothes and build strong houses.

A discussion of the wind could eventually lead into a discussion of the Three Little Pigs and why the first two houses were blown down.

Wind Experiments

On a windy day take your children outside and experiment with objects to see if they can be blown by the wind. Why does the wind move some things and not others? Observe the weight of the object or the strength of the wind. Here are some pairs of objects to compare:

a piece of paper and a book
a leaf and a tree
a balloon and a ball

End up with kites or balloons and let each child have one on a long string to watch as it soars through the sky. An interesting related activity would be to ask the children where they would go if the wind would give them one free ride.

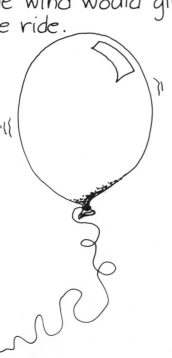

Kite Construction

Materials: Large plastic garbage bag, kite string, strong tape, thin rods or large straws.

cut plastic bag and lay flat

cut off each corner

make holes and reinforce with tape

1. Cut the garbage bag so that you can lay it out flat.
2. Cut off each corner as shown. Make a hole on each side. Reinforce the holes with strong tape.
3. Tape two thin rods or double straws down each side. (To make a rod from straws, slit one straw down about ½ inch at one end. Squeeze this end together and stick it into the end of another straw. Tape the two straws together in the middle.)
4. Tie one end of a 4-foot piece of string to one side of the kite and the other end to the other side. Tie your ball of string to the center of that string.

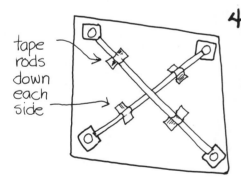

tape rods down each side

tie 4-foot string to each end

attach ball of string to center of 4-foot string

Wind Power

Moving air creates air power. Help your children recall ways that moving air makes things move. Discuss how a windmill and a sailboat work and what happens to a balloon that has been untied.

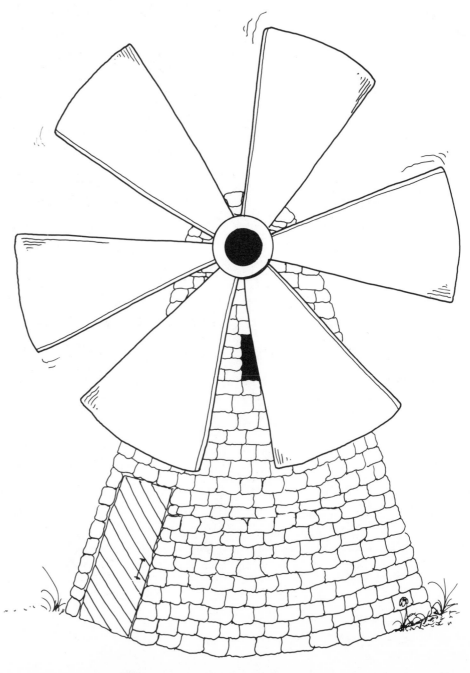

Rain Experiment

By conducting this simple experiment, you can show your children how rain is made.
Materials: Tea kettle, a pie pan, water, ice cubes.

1. Bring the water to a boil in the tea kettle. (Hold open the spout if it is the whistling kind.)

2. Place the pie pan filled with 5-10 ice cubes over the steam. Do not let children hold the pie pan. As water drops form, remove the pie pan from the steam and move it over so that your children can see what is happening.

fill pie pan with ice cubes

Encourage inquiry with such questions as: What has happened? Where did the water come from? How could the ice cubes affect the steam? When the water falls, what do we call it? Where did the steam (or water vapor) come from?

Explain briefly that the water on the earth, when it is warmed, turns into water vapor and rises into the sky, forming clouds. When the temperature of the clouds gets cold enough the vapor turns back into rain and falls to earth.

Making Rainbows

On a sunny day, you can help children find a rainbow by spraying water across the sun's rays with a garden hose. The rays of the sun contain all the colors mixed together, but the water acts as a prism and separates the colors.

Making Things Move

Playing in the water is a great time to observe how things can be made to move (or propelled) across the water. Ask your child if he or she can think of ways to propel an empty meat tray across the top of the water. She will probably notice that she can get the tray to move by moving the water around it. She might also discover that she can get it to move by blowing.

Make a sail by weaving a straw through two corners of a triangle. Attach the sail to the tray by poking a hole through the tray with a pencil and then inserting the straw. Blow on the sail to make the tray move faster.

If you have an old egg beater, you can let your child propel her boat through the water by beating the water behind the boat.

Underwater Exploration

You can make a simple underwater viewer for your child by cutting a section out of the middle of a plastic pop bottle and covering one end with plastic wrap. Secure the wrap with a large rubber band. Great for viewing underwater scenes at the ocean, in the wading pool, or the bathtub.

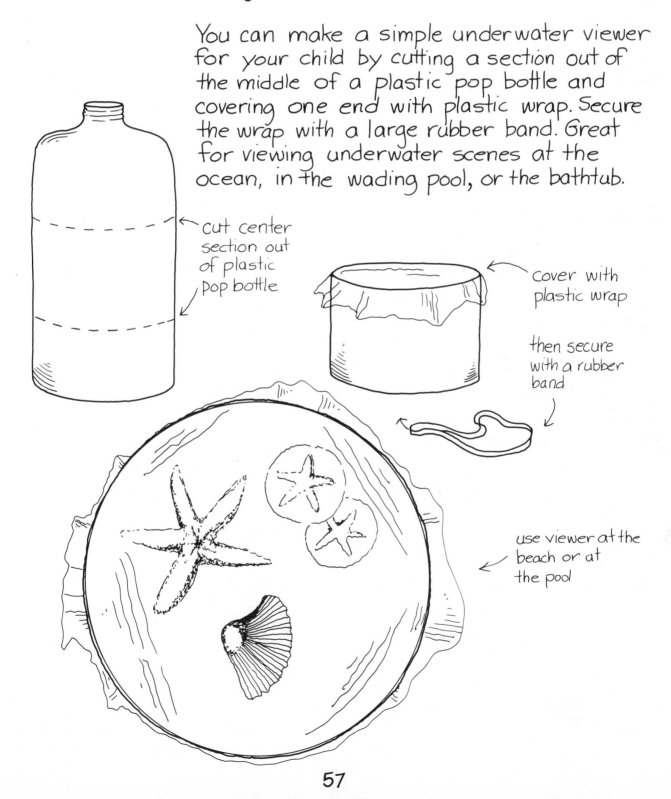

cut center section out of plastic pop bottle

cover with plastic wrap

then secure with a rubber band

use viewer at the beach or at the pool

Handmade Water Magnifier

cut inside out of lid

Make a small water magnifier out of a plastic container and lid for viewing small objects.
Materials: Plastic container and lid (margarine and cream topping containers are good), plastic wrap, penny, pairs of small objects.

1. Cut the inside out of the lid and the bottom out of the container itself.

cut bottom out of container

2. Lay a piece of plastic wrap over the rim of the container, place a penny in the center to pull it down a bit, then place the lid ring back on top.

3. Next pour water over the top, filling the plastic wrap. Remove the penny. (The slight sag of the plastic wrap will leave a curve on the bottom of the water, causing a magnification of objects placed beneath it.)

lay a piece of plastic wrap over rim and add penny; replace lid rim

4. Place a small object, like a penny, under the container and another one alongside. Let your children notice how the penny viewed through the water looks larger. Other small objects work equally well. It is easier for children to notice the enlargement if they have an identical object outside the container to compare it with.

remove penny and add water

place a small object under container

Four Seasons Plate

Have your children make season calendars with a paper plate. The calendar shows pictures of apple trees as they appear during the four seasons. Perhaps you can give each child four tree shapes to paste onto the plate and then let the children draw in blossoms for spring, leaves for fall and apples for summer, and leave the fourth tree bare with leaves or snow on the ground.

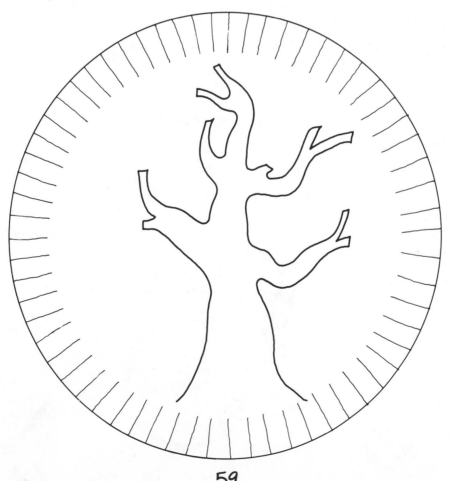

Discovery Walk

Each time you go on a walk with your children, turn it into a discovery walk. Add variety and dimension by changing the purpose or emphasis of each walk. Below is a list of things you and your children can look for on a walk around the block. Encourage your children to expand the list. Look for something different each day of the season.

animals
things with wheels
garbage
things in pairs
flowers
textures on buildings
signs with words
things that are tall
things that grow
smooth things
rough things
things that smell
sounds

signs of the seasons
old things
new things
things of different colors
things that start with
   a certain letter
things that blow on a
   windy day
things that have shadows
things that are shiny

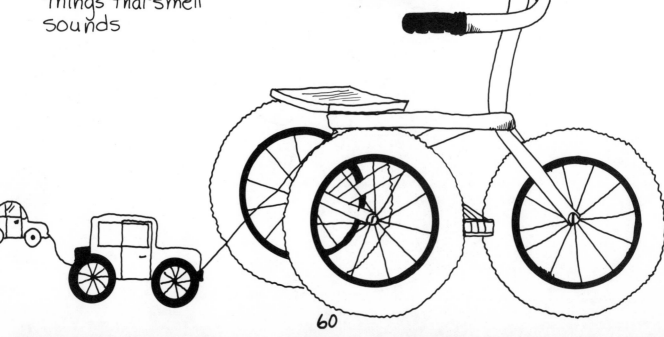

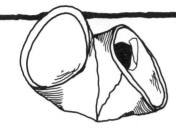

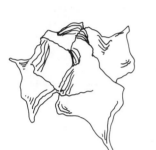

Garbage Poster

Let your children help in the recycling of paper, cans and bottles. Explain why we collect these items. One nice day, take the children on a garbage walk. Give them each an empty lunch sack and have them pick up garbage as they walk along. When you return, discuss how each piece spoils the environment. Let the children glue or tape their garbage onto a large piece of paper to make a garbage poster.

Surveys

Children love taking surveys. Find out how many children have brown shoes on, how many have white and so on. Make a simple graph showing how many in each category. If you run out of things to survey inside, look around outside. How many houses have flowers in bloom? How many children have animals at home? How many dogs? How many cats?

Our Shoes

7
6
5
4
3
2
1

BROWN   BLACK   TAN   OTHER

Star Experiment

Discuss stars with your children. Explain that stars are actually suns that are so far away that they appear small. We receive no real light or heat from these suns, we merely see them twinkle in the sky.

Why don't we see stars during the day? Set up a simple experiment with your children. Have them shine a flashlight in a room that is well lit. Next, turn off all lights and close all blinds. Make the room as dark as possible. Now have the children shine the flashlight. Can they see the light better? How does this experiment relate to the stars?

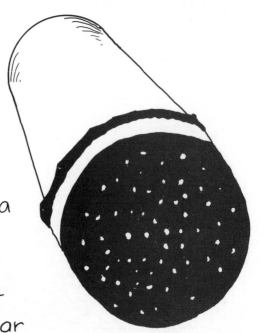

Star Scope

Show your children how to make a pretend star scope.

Materials: Cardboard tube, black paper, toothpick.

1. Tape a piece of black paper over the end of a cardboard tube.
2. Poke some holes in the paper with a toothpick.
3. Have a child point the tube towards a bright source of light and look up through the open end. The light shining through the holes will appear like stars in the night.

Smell Bottles

Use flavor concentrates to make smell bottles. Ask your pharmacist for eight small brown plastic pill containers with easy-to-remove plastic tops. In each bottle place a cotton ball. Drop two drops of flavor concentrate on each cotton ball. (You can find concentrates such as vanilla, peppermint extract, imitation butter, onion juice, and lemon extract in the baking supplies section of your supermarket.) You can make each bottle different, or you can have two bottles with the same smell and have the children match the pairs.

2 drops
of flavor
concentrate

place cotton
in bottle

Sound Bottles

Using familiar foods, you can help your children learn to distinguish like sounds. Ask a film shop salesperson for eight small film cans. Fill each can approximately ¼ full with the following pantry staples: two with salt, two with rice, two with flour, and two with macaroni. Secure the lids and mix up the cans. Using only their ears, your children must find the pairs of cans that sound the same.

FLOUR
RICE
MACARONI

Object Sounds

Set out four or five objects that make
different sounds in front of you and have
your children close their eyes. Tap
on one of the objects and see if
they can guess which object it was
by the sound it made. If you have
time, let your children take turns tapping
the objects.
   Make the game harder for older children by
just walking around the room and tapping on
random objects for them to guess.

Taping Sounds

A fun activity for young children is
identifying sounds. Tape record sounds that
would be familiar to your children. Later, use
the sound tape for a listening game. As you
play the tape, see how many of the sounds
the children can identify. Examples:
   musical instruments
   street noises (horns, footsteps, etc.)
   washing machine, dryer
   running water
   bells ringing (doorbell, school bell, etc.)
   alarm clock
   TV program
   Make the sounds hard or easy
to identify depending on the age
and ability of your children.

Sound Travels

You can show children how sound travels by conducting this simple sound experiment. Tie a metal spoon to a piece of string. Have your child hold the end of the string to her ear. Strike the spoon gently with another spoon. The sound of the two spoons hitting will travel up the string and the child should be able to hear the noise clearly.

Tin Can Telephones

Children today are still delighted with simple tin can telephones. You can make a set for your children with two empty tin cans that have smooth edges. Punch holes in the bottom of the cans. Thread twelve feet of wire through the holes. Wind each end in and out of a button, which acts as a stopper.

wind wire in and out of button

Two children use the phone by each holding one of the cans and stretching the wire as far as possible. One child talks into his can while the other child holds his can over his ear to listen. The vibrations travel along the taut wire.

poke holes in each can

Scales

Let your children experiment with scales.
Borrow a food scale and let them take
turns weighing apples, potatoes,
nuts, and such. Set up some
small problems. Examples: Find
out how many nuts equal the
weight of an apple. How many
nuts does it take to make
one pound?

Personal Weight

Children's natural interest in weighing
different objects usually leads to an
interest in weighing themselves. Let
your children take turns weighing
themselves on a bathroom scale.
Make a chart that compares their
weight with the weight of other
children, adults, and objects.

Homemade Scale

Materials: coat hanger, string, two large paper cups.

1. Cut out the middle section of the bottom wire on a coat hanger. Hang the coat hanger on a doorknob.
2. Cut out two equal lengths of string, 6 or 7 inches long.
3. Poke two holes across from each other at the top of each cup and tie the ends of the strings onto the cups to make handles.
4. Hook the handles over the ends of the wire hanger.
5. Have your children take turns measuring items to see if they weigh the same. Introduce the term balance.

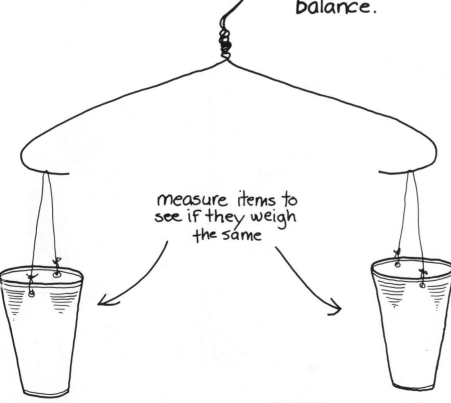

measure items to see if they weigh the same

Hand Prints

Materials: Paper, paint, brush.
Have your children paint the palms of their hands and make a print on a piece of paper. Make your own hand print next to each child's. Compare the prints. Discuss growing up and the changes that take place.

Mirror Anatomy

Children can practice naming the parts of their bodies while looking in a mirror. They will also enjoy practicing different facial expressions. Observing how they look when they have different feelings inside helps children to understand the "body language" of others.

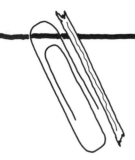

Measuring With Yarn

Children love to measure things. Give them a ruler, tape measure or yardstick and set them at tasks measuring the floor, tables, and such. To make a game, put pieces of yarn cut to the exact length of various objects in the room into a box. See if the children can figure out which piece of yarn goes with which object.

Measuring Ribbons

Cut leftover holiday ribbon into different lengths. Have your children find the longest ribbon, the shortest. Have them put all the ribbons in size order, starting with the shortest ribbon.

You can also cut the ribbons into four sets of two same-size ribbons each, but each set of ribbons a different length. Mix up all the ribbons, then have the children find those of equal length.

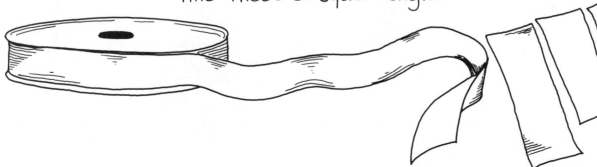

Texture Box

Collect fabric squares in a box. Let the children sort the squares by colors, patterns, and textures.

For a more advanced texture game, place two squares of five or six different textures in a bag. The children first reach in and pull out one square, then reach in again (without peeking) to find the other square that has the same texture. Examples of fabrics with distinctive textures:

    silk
    corduroy
    wool
    cotton
    flannel
    nylon
    seersucker

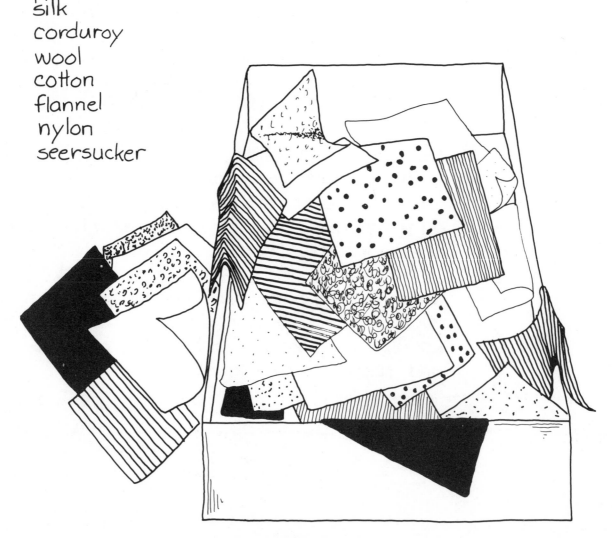

Texture Races

A block race is fun for young children and it also teaches them about textures and friction.

You need two long kindergarten blocks and a smooth piece of plywood or heavy cardboard. Lean one end of the board against the wall so that it slants down to the floor. To hold a race, two children each place a block at the top of the board and see whose block slides to the bottom the fastest. But there **is** some strategy involved: The child must first choose a square of fabric from the box described in the previous activity, and wrap it around the block. A safety pin will hold the fabric in place. Children will soon discover that blocks wrapped in smooth cloth will travel faster than blocks wrapped in a coarse material.

use a safety pin to hold fabric in place

wrap material around wood block

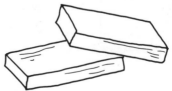

Snack Time Learning

Textures: Give your children a snack that contains something with a rough texture and something with a smooth texture. Help them distinguish between the two textures.

Dehydration: Discuss the differences between fresh fruit and dehydrated fruit (dehydrated, or dried, is drier and shrunken). Make your own raisins by cooking grapes on low heat overnight.

Counting: Play a counting game at snack time. You need some raisins and dice. Have your children take turns rolling one die and counting out the same number of raisins to eat.

Shapes: Whenever you have children make or eat a sandwich, have them notice how it has been cut. What shape was it before it was cut? What shape are the two halves? Can the sandwich be cut a different way to make two different shapes?

Snack Time Learning

Opposites: The difference between the terms **big** and **little** can be pointed out at snack time. Example: Some fruits have big seeds (pumpkins) while others have small seeds (apples).

Let your children make their own lemonade with a fresh lemon. After they have squeezed the lemon juice out of the lemon, let them taste the juice. Discuss how it tastes. Sour! Let the children add some sugar and ice water and stir. How does it taste now? Sweet!

Estimating: Let children estimate quantity. Example: Have them estimate how many cups of popped corn 1/4 cup of popcorn kernels will make, or how many seeds they will find in a pumpkin or an orange.

Changes: Observe the color and texture of vegetables before and after they are cooked. How do they change? Why?

Let your children make some flavored gelatin. Have them notice what happens to dry gelatin when it is mixed with boiling water. What effect does the cold temperature of the refrigerator have on the liquid Jello?

Make some butter with your children. Have them notice how the cream changes from a liquid to a solid. Any other changes? What about color?

Color-Coordinated Snacks

Help your children learn their colors
with color-coordinated snacks.

Green: lettuce, cucumbers, zucchini, peas,
   beans

Yellow: bananas, lemonade, yellow cake, corn

Orange: carrots, oranges, cooked pumpkin,
   cheddar cheese

White: milk, cottage cheese, yoghurt, bread

Red: tomatoes, ketchup, raspberry or cherry
   flavored drinks, gelatins, or jams, red apples

Brown: hot chocolate, peanut butter, whole
   wheat toast, chocolate cookies

Color Experiment

Materials: Yellow, red, and blue food coloring;
3 spoons; 3 clear glasses of water.

1. Hold up a clear glass filled with water. Let
   one child add a drop of yellow food coloring
   and stir the water. Ask, "What color did the
   water turn?"

2. Let another child add a drop of red food
   coloring to the glass of yellow water.
   Before adding the red, ask, "What color
   will the water turn now?" Most children
   will answer, "Red." Let the child add the red
   and stir. Point out that the water has turned
   orange, not red.

3. Let your children experiment with other
   primary color combinations.

Color Wheel

Young children can practice learning the names of colors by playing a simple color matching game.

Materials: Cardboard, marking pens, wooden snap clothespins.

1. Cut a circle 7 to 10 inches in diameter out of heavy cardboard.
2. Divide the circle into four sections. Color each section a different color-red, yellow, green, blue.
3. Color four clothespins to correspond to each color section.
4. The player matches a clothespin to a color section on the circle and attaches the clothespin to that section.

Color Scopes

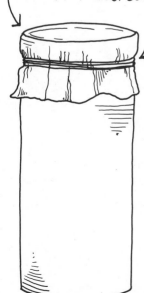

fold paper over viewer and secure with a rubber band

Children love viewing the world from behind these colored viewers.

Materials: Toilet paper rolls, colored cellophane paper, rubber bands.

1. Cut 4-inch squares out of red, yellow, and blue cellophane paper.
2. Fold a cellophane square over the end of a toilet paper roll. Secure it with a rubber band or tape.
3. Have the children experiment by placing both a red and a blue paper on the scope. Do you have a purple viewer? What about orange and green?

Sink or Float Experiment

Indoors or outside, let your children play in or around a tub of water. Give them objects to place in the water to see if they will sink or float. See if they can guess beforehand whether or not the objects will sink or float.

   Add salt to some water in a small container. Now what will sink or float in the water? Why will some things sink in plain water but not sink in the salted water?

place objects in water to see if they sink or float

Water Play

Water play is a good activity on an otherwise dull day. Fill a plastic dishpan halfway with warm water. Pour in a couple of drops of liquid dish detergent and a couple of drops (optional) of food coloring. Give your children straws with which to blow bubbles, dishes to wash, or cups to fill and refill. Let the children think of other things to play with in the water. You may want to have your children wear plastic aprons or old clothing.

Wave Machine

fill jar with two-thirds water

add drops of blue food coloring

Materials: Small glass or plastic jar with lid, water, blue food coloring, mineral oil.
1. Fill the jar two-thirds full with water.
2. Add a couple of drops of blue food coloring and mix well.
3. Fill up the rest of the jar with mineral oil. Get rid of as many air bubbles as you can. Secure the lid tightly.
4. The children should hold the bottle sideways and gently tip it, creating delightful wave actions.

fill jar with mineral oil

have children tilt bottle

Personal Clock

Children do not need to know how to tell time to understand that our lives are run on a cycle that is repeated every day. A personal clock can help illustrate.

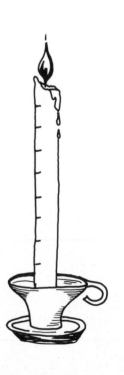

Make a circular chart with pictures of daily routine activities placed in their proper sequence. Be sure to put in all special activities for your child, such as a special TV time or a special story time. It is not necessary to mark the times on your chart unless you actually do the activity at a certain time each day. Attach a spinner to the chart so the child can move it around during the day as he does each activity.

Candle Clock

Measuring time is hard for young children to comprehend. Activities such as these help them to visualize the concept.

Materials: 2 candles that are the same length, ruler, paper, marker.

1. Burn one candle for 30 minutes.
2. Measure the difference in length between the two candles. This length now represents a half-hour.
3. Use the half-hour length to mark the rest of both candles. You can mark the hours with a longer mark.
4. Burn a candle for several hours. Have the children tell you how much time has passed by reading the calibrations marked earlier.

Sand Timer

Materials: 2 identical glass jars with lids, glue, sand.

1. Glue the tops of the jar lids together with a glue that will glue metal.
2. Hammer four medium-sized nail holes in the lids. Hammer two holes through one side of the lids and two holes through on the other side.
3. Fill one of the jars with sand (if you do not have sand, salt will work), then screw on the lids and the other empty jar.
4. Tip the jars over and time how long it takes for the sand to stop running. By adding or removing sand, try to get the timer to represent a standard unit of time (such as 1 or 2 minutes). Children can use this timer when playing games with others or by themselves. Children enjoy timers because they make "turns" seem more fair.